managing the risks of working alone

Personal safety advice for lone workers

SecuriCare International Limited

Martin House, Barley Rise, Strensall, York, England, YO32 5AA.
Telephone: +44 (0) 1904 492 442
Email: trainers@securicare.com
Website: www.securicare.com

ISBN: 978-0-9560159-5-2

Printed by Wood Richardson Ltd, Digital and Litho Printers,
Royden House, 156 Haxby Road, York, England, YO31 8EY

Copyright 2021. SecuriCare International limited.

All rights reserved. No part of this publication may be reproduced, stored in a retrieval system or transmitted in any form or by any means, electronic, mechanical, photocopying, recording, or otherwise, without prior permission of SecuriCare International Ltd.

Although great care has been taken in the production of this guidance to ensure accuracy, the Publishers cannot under any circumstances accept responsibility for errors, omissions or advice given in this publication.

managing the risks of working alone

Authors
Philip N Hardy
Trevor Platt
Karl Blackwell

Published by
SecuriCare International Ltd

CONTENTS:

Introduction
Definition of a Lone Worker
Employers Responsibilities
Preventing and Managing Work Related Violence
Dynamic Risk Assessment
Understanding and Preventing Conflict
Understanding the Causes of Changes in Behaviour
Communication Skills
Incident Management
The Use of Force

Introduction

Lone workers can face a greater risk of harm from workplace hazards due to the nature of their work. These hazards can include the location where the work is to take place and the route to get there, other people present at that location and any objects/items required for the work or already present at the location.

This book is designed to help lone workers, and employers of lone workers, to risk assess the working conditions and situations that may be encountered, to try to provide the safest possible working environment.

The information, guidance and support herein are supplied to ensure those working alone are best prepared before they embark, whilst travelling, when they are engaged with the customer and when they leave the venue.

Even when all foreseeable precautions are taken, situations can still change in unexpected ways, which is why it is important for all those involved to ensure they are working together to protect the safety of those working alone.

Definition of a Lone Worker

A lone worker is *"someone who works by themselves without close or direct supervision"* (Health & Safety Executive).

Here are a few examples of lone working:
- People who work from home
- People who work alone at a fixed base, e.g., in a shop, petrol station or warehouse
- People who work separately from other people or outside normal hours, e.g., security, cleaners or maintenance
- People who work away from a fixed base, e.g., health, medical and social workers visiting people's homes; delivery drivers, taxi drivers, couriers; postal staff, estate agents, sales representatives; agricultural or forestry workers
- Voluntary/charity workers

Lone workers can be directly employed, although many are independent contractors, freelancers, or self-employed. The work is often informal and on-demand, obtained through online platforms or delivered on a task-by-task basis. There may be a requirement to work to deadlines, visit remote/isolated domestic, commercial or industrial premises and there can often be additional risks related to the journeys to and from a location.

Employers Responsibilities

Working alone and/or in high-stress situations can negatively impact a person's stress levels and mental health. Working away from other colleagues and managers can mean support is difficult to achieve. Poor contact arrangements can make people feel disconnected, isolated or abandoned. Putting systems and procedures in place that encourage direct and regular contact between lone workers and their colleagues or management can help.

All these factors need to be considered when thinking about health, safety and welfare.

Employers have a legal duty towards lone workers under:
- The Health & Safety at Work Act
- The Management of Health & Safety Regulations

Before allowing people to work alone employers are required to think about and deal with any Health and Safety risks that we may be exposed to. These areas of risk include:
- Travelling to and from the venue
- The venue and its occupants
- Angry, aggressive, or violent behaviours
- Systems for monitoring/supervising lone workers
- Keeping in touch and responding to incidents

Employers must assess and control the risks in the workplace. They must identify what might cause harm to people and ensure they are doing enough to prevent harm. If they employ more than 5 workers this must be in the form of a written statement/policy. This should include the following:
- The hazard: what are the things that may cause harm?
- How these things may harm people: e.g., physically, mentally, emotionally
- What is being done to control these risks: e.g., training, personal alarms, tracking devices
- A process for regularly reviewing this assessment

Risk Assessment and Control Measures

Whether conducted as a separate lone worker risk assessment or included in general risk assessments, employers must take steps to control risks where necessary. This must include:
- Consultation with those required to work alone to identify risks and the required control measures
- Implementing guidance, instructions, training and supervision
- Taking steps to remove risk where possible
- Review risk assessments periodically and update any significant changes

The People
Employers must take into consideration any possible impact on the risk posed by the lone worker or other people who may be involved during the fulfilment of the work:
- How experienced is the lone worker?
- Have they received training?
- Is there anything that makes them more vulnerable? Are they young, pregnant, disabled, or inexperienced?
- Who are they expected to meet and does this increase the risk?
- Could they encounter other people when travelling to, or whilst visiting the designated venue that would increase the risk?

The Environment
Is there anything relating to the environment or venue that impacts the risk?
- How will the lone worker get to the venue and are there any risks associated with travelling to and from there?
- Are there any heightened risks associated with the venue? E.g., high crime rate, previous incidents or poor phone reception
- Is the venue isolated or difficult to access?

Equipment
They must consider if the safety of the lone worker would be improved or compromised by the addition or absence of specific equipment:
- Does the lone worker need/have adequate and reliable means of communication?
- Is there an effective method of calling for help or assistance?
- Is PPE needed? E.g., protective clothing/gloves, body-cam, personal alarm, stab/slash-proof vest

Task or Role
Could the job role or the task increase the risk?
- Are rules or sanctions being enforced/imposed?
- Are there any cash transactions involved?
- Is it necessary to remove/restrict access to goods or property?
- Will there be a need to deliver a negative or distressing message?

Preventing and Managing Work Related Violence

Working alone does not automatically imply there is a greater risk of experiencing angry, aggressive or violent behaviour, but it does make us more vulnerable if it does occur.

Any form of abuse or violence against lone workers is unacceptable and could seriously affect our psychological and physical health. Training in conflict management and personal safety will help lone workers recognise potential risks and help us take appropriate action to eliminate or reduce these risks.

There are specific areas that need to be considered when developing a strategy for preventing and managing the risk of angry, aggressive or violent behaviours.

Preparation

Anyone required to work alone in the community or visit domestic or commercial premises should receive adequate training and have access to any information they may need to prepare them for the role or task they will be required to perform. To help us to prepare we should consider any or all of the following:
- How will we get there? Are there any known risks associated with travelling to and from the venue?
- What time of the day will we be required to travel?
- Does the weather present a hazard?
- Up to date information about the location and any known risks
- Any potential triggers to conflict or other hazardous behaviours and how to avoid them
- Is there any known history of abusive, aggressive or violent behaviour by the person/people at the venue?
- How will we call for help or assistance?
- What help or assistance will be available?
- What can we do until help or assistance arrives?

If we have prepared for all the known risks associated with an activity and considered the possible unknown risks, we will be better prepared to act safely should an incident occur. Knowing it is possible to call for help, the form of help that is available and how long it will take for the help to arrive will make it easier for anyone requiring assistance to keep calm and continue to manage the situation.

Having prepared and planned for the travel, activity or task, we will need to continually assess for any risks that may occur.

Dynamic Risk Assessment

We all risk assess consciously or subconsciously as we go about our lives and make decisions based on our instincts, fears or analysis of the things happening around us.

Arriving at the Venue

Questions a lone worker should be asking themselves when arriving at the venue include:
- Are there any visible risks? Is the area poorly lit; is there damage to property or vehicles; are there other people around or in the venue that give cause for concern?
- If travelling by car, is there a safe parking place/space?
- Is it possible to park in a position where there is easy access to the vehicle and be able to drive away? E.g., face out of, not into, a cul-de-sac
- Is there a phone signal?
- Before entering the venue plan a route out and back to the vehicle, public transport, or a public place where there are other people
- Is access to the location via a lift or stairs; which is the best option?
- Is there any reason to be concerned about entering the venue? E.g., shouting or arguing; does the venue look safe to enter?
- Do the occupants give any reason for concern? E.g., do they smell of alcohol; do they appear injured or distressed; is there any indication they have been using drugs or other illegal substances; is there reason to be concerned about their mental or physical health?

If there is *any reason* to feel uneasy about continuing the visit and entering the venue, *act immediately*. Remember, it is always possible to return there another time.

Inside the Venue

Having decided it is safe to enter a venue, it's important to keep assessing and making decisions:
- Pre-plan an excuse/reason to terminate the activity/task; keep it plausible and make it time-sensitive, facilitating the need to leave immediately
- Continue to assess the route out of the venue
- Check if the entrance/exit is locked or barred
- Is the venue safe? Are there animals, items or objects that are harmful or dangerous?
- Are there any other people in the venue that were not expected or give cause for concern?
- It is advised not to remove footwear; take shoe covers to be used as an alternative
- Decline the offer of drinks/food
- Sit on the edge of the chair/sofa and as close as possible to the exit route
- If the need arises for assistance or emergency services, how can they be contacted without alerting the occupant(s)?

Calling for Help

Calling for help or assistance is not something that anybody wants to have to do, but there may be times when it is necessary, so a robust plan needs to be in place. It may be important for this call to be made without alerting other individuals in attendance, or to openly make the call and mask its true intention.

Some options are:
- Have a number ready on speed-dial/re-call that can be activated discreetly so that someone can listen in, e.g., a designated manager or colleague
- If a call can be made safely, can the person who answers gather information without further compromising the safety of the person needing help?
- On iPhone's, pressing the power button five times rapidly will automatically call the emergency services. Android phones have an emergency button on the lock screen allowing calls to be made even when the phone is locked

The use of a *CODE WORD* or phrase is a good way of initiating the process, e.g. "Hi, this is (NAME), I am calling to let you know I will be late for my next appointment. Could you tell *THE SUPPORT SUPERVISOR* please?"

The *CODE WORD* should start the emergency information gathering process. There needs to be a written *SCRIPT* that is followed, e.g.:

Assistant: "Do you need help?"	**Caller:** "Yes, that's right"
Assistant: "Do you need the Police?"	**Caller:** "Yes, that's right"
Assistant: "Are you at (address)?"	**Caller:** "Yes, that's right"
Assistant: "Is the person armed?"	**Caller:** "Yes/No"
Assistant: "Are you injured?"	**Caller:** "Yes/No"
Assistant: "Help is on its way"	**Caller:** "Thank you, I will let you know"

It is vital that EVERYONE knows the CODE WORD and the SCRIPT.

As lone workers, any of us can find ourselves in situations where we need assistance, which is why we require training in conflict management and personal safety. This will give us the skills needed to reduce antagonism and de-escalate the situation if possible, or take steps to help protect ourselves from harm or injury until help arrives.

Understanding and Preventing Conflict

By far the best way to deal with difficult, angry or aggressive individuals, is to make a positive interaction/intervention as early as possible. The earlier we deal with the underlying problem, concern or frustration, the less chance there is of the behaviour escalating. To effectively manage difficult people, it is important to explore and understand the causes and functions of behaviour.

To understand how situations develop, let's take a closer look at what influences people's moods or feelings.

What a person thinks about the situation will affect how they feel, and if they feel strongly enough about the situation, this change in their emotional state can lead to a change in how they behave towards others. Their attitude and behaviour will in turn influence how others act and behave towards them; this is referred to as the Betari Box Theory and the following diagram is sometimes called the Betaris Box.

By positively changing our behaviour and attitude the behaviour of others will naturally change as well.

In short, our feelings and attitude will directly influence our behaviour towards others, and this will affect how they feel and behave towards us. This emphasises the need to interact in a positive way.

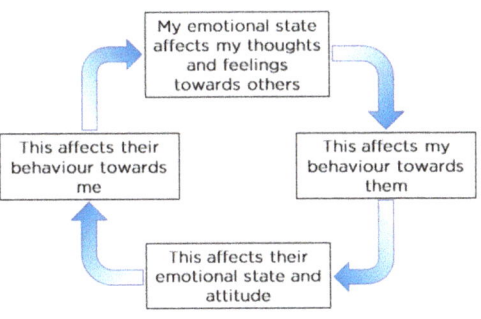

Understanding the Causes of Changes in Behaviour

There will always be people who are difficult to interact with, but the majority of people are quite reasonable and only express negative feelings and behaviour when they feel upset, aggrieved or frustrated by their circumstances, or someone else's attitude or actions.

How a person feels and responds to their circumstances can be the result of experiences and events that take place over hours, days, weeks, months, or even years. We are not usually in a position to help with the long-term influences affecting their current emotional or mental state, we can, however, help them through their current circumstances and/or issue. If we engage with the person with an empathic approach based on the assumption that their behaviour is only happening for a reason, we are much more likely to have a positive interaction.

The following Iceberg Theory illustrates how long, medium, and short-term influences all contribute to a person reaching a crisis point. Most of these influences are unknown or are not visible to us, but by recognising when a person has reached a crisis point, our next interaction could determine whether or not their behaviour escalates or de-escalates.

Iceberg Theory

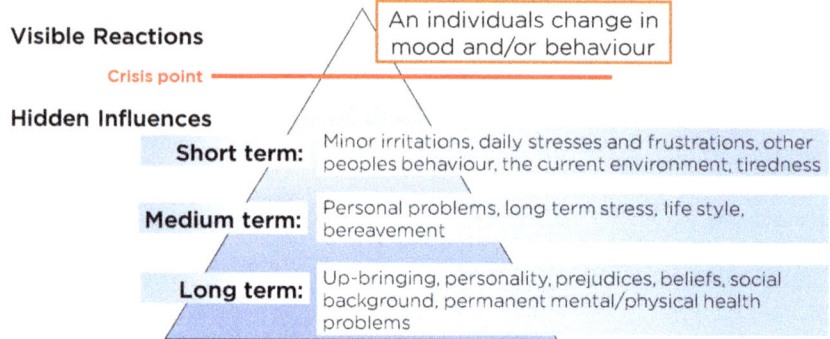

Patterns of Behaviour

There are some people who can go from calm to violent in a very short period; thankfully very few people fit this profile and most people follow a similar pattern of escalation as their feelings and behaviour change.

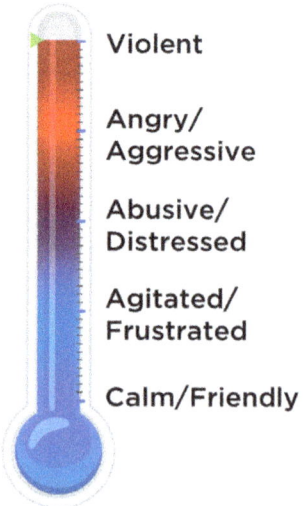

When people are in a state of calm we normally find them easy to get on with, which makes communication easier. When someone is frustrated, distressed or angry, however, we need to think carefully about how we communicate with them. Events beyond our control may cause people's behaviour to escalate; this might mean the person is agitated before we meet them. Most people's behaviour will not escalate any further than the angry stage, because of their ability to manage and regulate their behaviour, or because of the possible consequences that might arise if they allow their behaviour to escalate any further. It is therefore important to be able to recognise the changes in a person's mood or behaviour when their feelings are expressed negatively.

Having identified that a person is unhappy or angry, an early, positive interaction/intervention will make it easier to control events and de-escalate the situation. Remember, a person who has become angry and abusive may take some time to return to a state of calm, so any further interaction/intervention will need to be carefully managed.

We should try to ensure that we do not expect, and therefore invite negative behaviour.

We should always try to:
- Be non-judgemental and do not make assumptions about people just because of how they look or behave
- Remember, behaviour always happens for a reason; try to understand why the person is behaving as they are
- Believe that a positive outcome is possible
- Accept that mistakes can and do happen and that the person may have a genuine reason for being upset or angry
- Look for ways to rectify things in a positive way

Most incidents will be resolved amicably and by communicating effectively with the person.

Communication Skills

Communicating with others is a skill that most of us use every day. Some people are better communicators than others, but the majority of us get it right most of the time. When communication fails people get confused, upset, frustrated or even angry.

Communication can be described as "the sharing of information" or "the imparting of a message" involving both a *transmitter* (the person sending the message) and a *receiver* (the person receiving the message).

How We Communicate

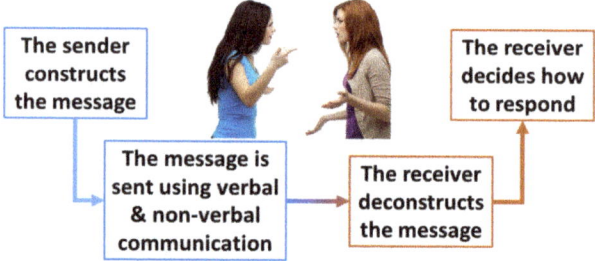

It's not what you say but HOW you say it!

Both the person "transmitting the message" and the person "receiving the message" will be subconsciously influenced by the others non-verbal communication as well as the content of the verbal message.

According to the British Journal of Social and Clinical Psychology, the messages we send are comprised of three parts: *words, tone of voice*, and *body language*.

This chart displays the influence that each of these parts plays in the communication process. This demonstrates that 93 % of the messages we transmit or receive is made up of body language and tone of voice. People will determine our true feelings towards them from how we appear and our tone of voice more than the actual words we speak.

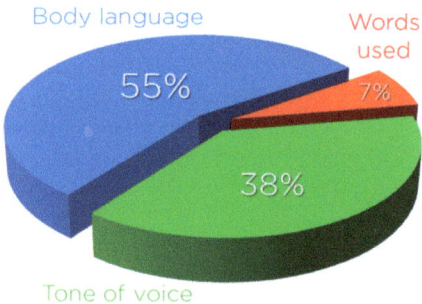

Body language or non-verbal communication includes:
- Facial expressions
- Eye contact
- Posture or stance
- Positioning of hands
- Personal space (proximity)
- Clothing or appearance
- Touch
- Gestures

When interacting with other people we need to consider the effect that our body language and our presence is having. When speaking, we must control our tone of voice and avoid raising our voice, shouting, or talking too quickly.

Barriers to Communication

We may sometimes come up against barriers to communication; factors that the environment or individuals bring to the situation that have an impact on the communication process. Even good communication can be disrupted or blocked by potential barriers.

Barriers to communication fall into three main categories:

Environmental Barriers:
The setting within which the conversation is taking place can affect how successful the communication process is. Environmental barriers include:
- The distance between the people trying to communicate
- Any physical barrier such as a screen or partition
- Lots of people talking at the same time
- The level of activity happening whilst we are trying to communicate
- Background noise/sounds
- Distractions
- Lighting

Personal Barriers:
Interpersonal and intrapersonal barriers refer to the human factors that could create a barrier to effective communication.

Interpersonal communication is between two or more people and relates to how well we communicate with others. It includes both verbal and non-verbal communication. It also involves listening and understanding the other person's perspective, how well we can problem solve and negotiate, and our ability to be assertive and make decisions.

Intrapersonal communication is between you and yourself and relates to emotional intelligence. It includes self-confidence and discipline, our self-awareness and how we conceive ourselves, our ability to concentrate and focus and overcome distractions.

Cultural Barriers:
Culture can be defined as "a particular social group or organisation characterised by a defined look, mindset, attitude or behaviour". Cultural groups can be organised on the grounds of:
- Age
- Education
- Social status
- Race
- Religion
- Political beliefs
- Personal values
- Gender
- Economic position
- Health
- Beauty
- Popularity

Overcoming Barriers to Communication

The first step to overcoming barriers to communication is to ensure that we don't introduce any barriers ourselves. The following steps are offered as a way of optimising the communication process.

Listening:
Active Listening involves more than just hearing the words a person is saying, it's also about being able to understand what the person means.

Not only do we need to listen, but we also need to be able to convince the other person that we are listening and understand what they are saying. A person is less likely to complain if we can demonstrate that we are listening, are interested in what they have to say, and they believe we are trying to help.

We need to allow the person time to explain their point of view without interrupting them, even if we don't agree with what they are saying. Often people simply need to talk to someone to help them release some internal frustration or anger. We should always focus on what they say, rather than how it makes us feel.

Asking Questions:
There are two types of questions that we can use: **Open** and **Closed**.

Open questions invite the person to communicate freely, allowing them to express themselves and allowing them to release any internal frustrations or anger. They ask the person to think and reflect, give their opinions and express their feelings.

Closed questions can be used to restrict the person's responses by limiting them to a simple "yes" or "no" answer, which can help us to control the tone and direction of the conversation. Closed questions allow us more time to speak and explain things in a calm, positive, and helpful manner.

Clarifying:
Using clarifying statements is a way of ensuring that everyone involved in the conversation understands the issues and the possible outcomes. They allow us to demonstrate that we have listened and can offer a solution.

Summarising:
To conclude a conversation, we can summarise what has been discussed and the possible solutions, options, or outcomes available.

Despite our best efforts, there are times when these techniques fail to prevent the situation from escalating to a more hazardous level.

However, by attempting to communicate, by listening, and by demonstrating a willingness to help, our interaction should be seen as a positive one, which will if nothing else, promote positive witnessing.

Incident Management

There are common warning signs that a person is becoming agitated or angry, such as arguing or raising their voice, staring, suddenly standing, invading personal space or pushing and shoving. We also need to be aware of any sudden changes in mood or lack of responses to questions; sometimes a person may just go quiet or stop communicating.

We need to follow our instincts; if the situation or the person(s) involved are creating an unsafe environment we need to consider leaving the area. Where there is a risk of physical violence, personal safety becomes the overriding priority.

Dealing with a high-stress situation involving aggressive, threatening or violent behaviours will have an additional impact on everyone involved.

Managing the Fight or Flight Response

When faced with angry or threatening behaviour, or asked to do something we may not be comfortable doing, we usually experience the effects of stress to some degree. The human body's natural response to stress is to either fight the threat or run away from it, hence the term "Fight or Flight".

The stress response is a primitive survival response that prepares us to act decisively to any developing danger or immediate perceived threat. It is a normal and natural response and can occur to differing degrees of intensity depending upon the situation and our past experiences. Although most of us rarely experience life-threatening situations in modern life, this primitive survival response still occurs when we perceive we are in danger or when we are being threatened.

The Effects of Stress

The symptoms of stress can be many and varied and they can affect people in many different ways. Some of the more common effects include:

Visual effects:
- Agitation
- Difficulty speaking
- Muscular tension
- Sweating
- Breathing faster
- Pupils dilate
- Shaking
- Red-faced

Hidden effects of Stress:
- Adrenaline rush
- Blood is diverted away from the digestive system, causing feelings of nausea or sickness
- Dry mouth
- Loss or reduction of peripheral vision
- Heart rate increases
- Thinking becomes difficult or focused on the threat

Experiencing stress symptoms is not a sign of failure or an indication that we are not capable of performing our job, it is simply an indicator that we are dealing with a challenging or stressful situation and our body is registering and responding to this.

These changes are caused, in part, by the release of **adrenaline** into the bloodstream. One crucial effect this has is on our ability to reason with common sense. The brain finds it harder to control rational thought and is more prone to instinctive responses.

The key is to try to stay or at least appear, **calm**. The following techniques can be used to help manage the stress response.

Anticipate Difficulties:
With training and experience, we can learn to anticipate some of the difficulties and challenges that we could face and therefore be better prepared in the event of them occurring.

Controlled Breathing:
By taking a deep breath and breathing out slowly, we can reduce stress in two ways:
- It supplies the brain with more oxygen to help optimise thinking capacity
- The regulation of the breathing process will help to facilitate relaxation

Try to Relax Muscular Tension:
Muscular tension can promote negative thinking, which can result in the sustained release of stress hormones. By relaxing and loosening muscle tension we:
- Become more relaxed physically, which will help us to think more clearly
- Our body language will become more relaxed. This will mean the non-verbal signals we are sending out will be more conducive to calming and de-escalation

Mental Distance:
It is easy to become personally and emotionally involved in an incident, especially if the abuse or threats are directed towards us. We should:
- Try to keep a "mental distance" by focusing on the situation and solutions and not the behaviour and the people involved
- Remember, despite what they may be saying, we are probably not the cause of the person's change in mood or behaviour

De-Escalation
De-escalation can be looked at in three phases, the Calming Phase, Building Rapport, and Reaching a Positive Conclusion.

Calming Phase:
To begin to de-escalate a difficult situation we must first instil an element of calm.

We can do this by allowing the person time or space and by moving away if necessary.

Adopt a relaxed and open posture by standing slightly to one side, at 45°. Our hands should be kept open and between us and the person. When talking remember to maintain an even tone and pitch and speak slowly.

When we have demonstrated our ability to stay calm, and have calmed the person down, we can begin to build a rapport with them.

Building Rapport:
Using the techniques discussed in Communication Skills can help us to build a rapport with the person. Remember, sometimes people have a genuine reason for being frustrated and angry and just need to have someone listen, empathise and offer help.

Reaching a Positive Conclusion:

Reaching a positive conclusion can sometimes just mean that we have not made a situation any worse. Hopefully, the majority of the time incidents will end positively. To help this process we should be clear when someone's behaviour is unacceptable. State what is achievable to help maintain realistic expectations. This may help them re-evaluate their position and look for an amicable solution rather than continue to lead the situation to a negative conclusion.

The Use of Force

In some unfortunate circumstances, we may have to use physical force to leave an incident/location or to protect ourselves; it is important to remember that the action taken will be judged on the following basis:

"was the action taken reasonable and necessary in all the circumstances?"

Section 3 Criminal Law Act 1967 states that:
"A person may use such force as is reasonable in the circumstances"

What is Reasonable and Necessary?

The use of force is only ever reasonable and necessary if all other non-physical strategies have been exhausted or discounted.

Non-physical strategies may include:
- Asking the person to stop what they are doing
- Trying to resolve any conflict
- Removing or reducing any source of frustration
- Taking evasive action such as moving away/leaving

The use of force may be justified if it is being used:
- When acting to save a life or protect an individual from harm or danger
- When acting in self-defence
- To prevent a crime
- To protect property

There are a variety of reasons why force must only be used as a last resort, including:
- Its use can create an increased risk of harm and injury to all those involved
- It increases the risk of allegations
- It could lead to legal action

Was the Force Used Proportionate to the Harm to be Avoided?

The amount or degree of force required will depend on several factors, including:
- The size or strength differences between the people involved
- The number of people who are involved
- The presence of any weapons
- A direct or explicit threat to cause immediate harm
- An increase in the resistance or violence used

Remember, even in the most difficult circumstances there are other options and actions available.

1. **Communication**: continue to try to communicate safely with the person
2. **Attracting attention**: attempt to raise the alarm without increasing the risk
3. **Compliance**: allow the situation to continue until a better opportunity arises, provided there is no immediate risk of harm
4. **Self-defence**: take the actions necessary to protect oneself from harm

Summary

People who present behaviours that are challenging, threatening or hazardous can be encountered anywhere and can be from any social, ethnic or economic group. The experience of working alone can bring an extra dimension to the problem of managing difficult or dangerous situations.

Legislation and penalties exist to deter most people from becoming aggressive or worse, however, a minority can go too far and create situations that may require us to make difficult decisions and sometimes put ourselves at risk.

We hope the knowledge and advice offered in this book will help and support people who work alone to interact with difficult and aggressive people more effectively and help keep everyone safe.

Notes

www.ingramcontent.com/pod-product-compliance
Lightning Source LLC
Chambersburg PA
CBHW062114290426
44110CB00023B/2817